Great Ghosts

Great Ghosts

DANIEL COHEN
Illustrated by DAVID LINN

SCHOLASTIC INC.
New York Toronto London Auckland Sydney

ISBN 0-590-45108-1

12 11 10 9 8 7 6 5 4 3 2   1 2 3 4 5 6/9

Printed in the U.S.A.   28

First Scholastic printing, October 1991

Contents

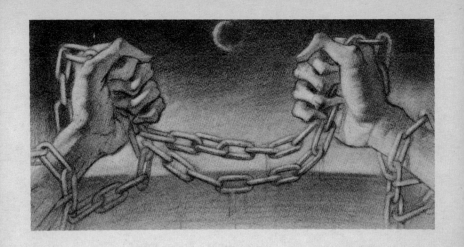

An Ancient Ghost

About two thousand years ago a writer in ancient Rome recorded this story. It is one of the oldest ghost stories we know.

There was a house in the city of Athens, Greece, that was said to be haunted. People who stayed the night heard moans and the clanking of chains. Then a horrible phantom appeared. It was an old man with long hair and a long beard. His clothes were little more than rags. From his thin arms and legs hung heavy chains. The phantom moaned and shrieked and shook his heavy chains. The sight was a terrifying one. Worse still, all those who saw the ghost were said to have nothing but bad luck afterward.

As you might imagine, not many people would stay in such a house. One look at the phantom would send them running into the street. If they heard the story, they would not rent the house. It was almost always empty.

One day a famous, but poor, scholar came to Athens to study. He was looking for a quiet place to live. But he had very little money. He saw the empty house, and asked how much it would cost to rent. The rent was very low indeed. It seemed to be just what he was looking for.

Still, the scholar knew there must be a reason why the house would rent so cheaply. He asked about it. At first, those renting the house avoided the question. But finally, the scholar was told about the ghost. The story didn't bother him. He was not a man to be easily frightened. He decided to take the house anyway.

On his first night in the house the scholar sat up late reading as usual. Then he began to hear noises like the rattling of chains, and moans. At first, they were soft, but they grew louder and louder. The scholar kept reading. He didn't pay any attention to the noises. He refused to have his studies interrupted.

Finally, the horrible figure itself appeared before him. The scholar couldn't ignore it any longer. But he wasn't frightened either. He stared at the phantom. The horrible figure moaned and screamed. The chains on its bony arms rattled and clanked. Still, the scholar just looked at it calmly.

After a few moments the scholar realized the ghost was not trying to frighten him. It wanted to get his attention. It wanted him to do something. The bony arms were not waving wildly. The ghost was motioning to the scholar. The scholar rose from his chair and followed the ghastly figure.

The ghost led him to a spot outside the house. There it pointed to the ground, gave its chains one more frantic shake, and disappeared. The scholar marked the spot, and went to bed.

Next morning he went to city officials and told them what he had seen. He said that they should dig at the spot the ghost had pointed out. They did, and found a human skeleton just a few feet beneath the surface. Ancient and rusted chains clung to the bones. These remains were collected and given a proper burial. The grim phantom in chains never again troubled the house.

The Man in Grey

The ghostly figure of a young man wearing the clothes of 250 years ago has often been seen in the balcony of one of London's oldest theaters, the Theatre Royal.

The figure wears a powdered wig and a three-cornered hat. What most people notice first is the long, grey cloak. He is called the Man in Grey. The hilt of a sword can be seen sticking out from beneath the cloak. Many fashionable young men dressed that way in London two and a half centuries ago. Many of them carried swords as well.

There is nothing really frightening about this ghost. He does not moan or howl. He does not even appear at night. The Man in Grey is usually seen in the afternoon or early evening. That's the time rehearsals are going on. He's seen mainly by the actors or members of the stage crew. Occasionally, he has been seen when there is an afternoon performance at the theater. People in the audience think the figure must be an actor in costume. The actors know better. The figure walks across the balcony and seems to disappear into the wall. Once or twice he has been seen backstage, or on the stage itself.

Far from being afraid of this phantom, most theater people look upon the Man in Grey as a sign of good luck. This particular ghost appears only at hit shows. If a show is going to be a flop, the Man in Grey is nowhere to be seen. People in the theater begin to worry when this ghost doesn't show up.

Several actors at the Theatre Royal have reported that they

were helped by this ghost or at least by some ghost. A young actress named Doreen Duke was auditioning for a part. Before going on, she was struck with stage fright. She felt paralyzed, unable to remember her lines or even move. Then she felt a friendly pat on the back. That broke the stage fright. When she turned around to see who had helped her, no one was there. She went out, had a good audition, and got the part. She always said she could never have done it without that pat from an unseen hand.

Another actress said that during a show, an invisible force moved her around the stage. Because of that, she gave a better performance.

Who is the Man in Grey? Some say he is the ghost of either Arnold Woodruffe or Thomas Hallam. They were actors killed in the theater by a fellow actor who went mad. Most actors doubt this. They say that the Man in Grey was a member of the audience, not a performer.

A more popular candidate is an unknown young man whose skeleton was found in the theater in 1860. Workmen broke through a wall and found it hidden there. The skeleton had a dagger sticking between its ribs. No one knows the identity of the skeleton. No one knows what happened, either. The most common explanation is that the young man was killed in a fight. His body was then bricked up in a hole in the wall of the old theater. A lot of people suspect that whoever he was, his ghost is now called the Man in Grey. He must have really loved the Theatre Royal because he has never left.

The Berkeley Square "Horror"

Today, No. 50 Berkeley Square in London is an ordinary bookstore. There is nothing unusual or terrifying about it— now. A century ago it was one of the most feared places in England.

Strangely, no one knows when or how the tales of the Berkeley Square "Horror" began. No one even knows what the thing was supposed to be. All people knew was that no one could spend a night alone in an upstairs room in the house and remain alive—and sane. By morning, people who had been in the room had either died of fright, or gone mad from sheer terror. Even the living were not able to speak of what they had seen.

Sir Robert Warboys didn't believe the stories. This bold fellow boasted that he would spend a night in the upstairs room. Sir Robert took his pistol with him. A group of his friends stood guard on the first floor. He said that if anything went wrong, if he felt he was in danger, he would pull a cord that would ring a bell on the first floor. His friends, who were all armed, would then come to his rescue.

Sir Robert had been in the room for about forty-five minutes when the bell on the first floor began to jangle wildly. His friends rushed upstairs. Before they got to the room they heard a shot. The door was locked and had to be broken down. Inside the room Sir Robert was slumped over the bed—dead.

His face was frozen in terror. He had died from fright. A bullet hole was found in the wall. There was no sign of what he had been shooting at. No one else in the house saw or heard anything.

One morning the maid of a family that rented No. 50 Berkeley Square was found in the upstairs bedroom. She had gone completely mad. All she could say was, "Don't let it touch me!" She died in the hospital a few weeks later.

Because of stories like that, the house was hard to rent. It was usually empty. In 1887, a couple of sailors, Edward Blunden and Robert Martin, were roaming the streets of London. They had lost all their money, and had no place to sleep. They wandered into Berkeley Square and saw the empty house at No. 50. It was starting to rain, so they broke into the house to spend the night. They didn't know anything about the place. The sailors explored the house. They thought the bedroom on the second floor was the best room in which to spend the night.

Martin fell asleep at once. Blunden was uneasy and couldn't sleep. He didn't know why. Then he heard footsteps and scratching noises outside the door. These noises fright-

ened him and he woke Martin. The men saw something large, dark, and shapeless enter the room. It made soft, hissing noises.

Blunden grabbed a chair to use as a weapon against the nameless terror. Martin darted through the open door and down the stairs. Outside he found a policeman and told him what had happened. The policeman knew No. 50 Berkeley Square all too well. He knew there was no time to lose. The two rushed back to the house.

They were too late. At the bottom of the stairs they found Blunden's body. He had fallen and broken his neck. His face wore a look of utter terror. He had been running away from something. But what?

The Screaming Skull

At a farmhouse in the country of Dorset in England, the owners keep a human skull on the table in the living room. They don't want to keep the skull there. They are just afraid to get rid of it.

The skull is said to be that of a servant who had been born in the West Indies. The servant never liked England. Before he died, he said that his spirit would not rest until his body was taken back to his native land.

This was not done. He was given a regular burial in the local churchyard. After that, all sorts of strange things began to happen. Terrible screams were heard coming from the grave. Horrible noises came from the room in which the servant had lived. On the farm, crops began to wither and cattle became sick and some died.

Finally, the servant's body was dug up and brought back to the house. The screaming stopped. Crops and cattle began to recover. However, the people in the house didn't like having a body around. They tried to rebury it several times. Each time the screams and other noises were heard again. And again there were crop failures and the mysterious death of cattle. So long as the body remained in the churchyard, the farm suffered from bad luck.

Finally, the owners of the farm gave up. They decided to keep the remains in the house. By now there was only a skeleton left. Over the years, bits and pieces of the skeleton disappeared. Today, only the skull remains.

From time to time new owners of the farm have tried to

get rid of the skull. It never worked. Whenever it was removed from its usual place, the skull screamed, and bad luck followed.

Another skull is kept at a place called Wardley Hall in England. This skull is said to belong to a man named Roger Downes, who lived and died three hundred years ago. He was a wild young man, who had his head cut off during a fight. The head was sent home to his sister at Wardley Hall. Since then it has never left for very long.

It's not that the people of Wardley Hall haven't tried to get rid of the skull. They often have. It has been buried, burned, and thrown in the river. But the next day it is always back in the little cabinet behind the stairs where it was kept in the first place. At least that is what the legends say.

According to a more recent story, a couple of visitors once stole the skull while no one was looking. They dropped it in a pond near the Hall. That night there was a terrible storm. Wardley Hall was struck by lightning. The roof was set on fire. The next morning the owners of Wardley Hall demanded that the visitors tell them what happened to the skull. They then went to the pond, fished out the skull, and put it back in its usual place.

Today, the owners of the Hall won't even allow the skull to be touched. They are deathly afraid of what might happen if it is taken away again.

The *Flying Dutchman*

In the era of the wooden sailing ships, the trip around the southern tip of Africa, called the Cape of Good Hope, was a very dangerous one. It was a place where violent storms could blow up suddenly. Many ships were caught in storms and disappeared without a trace.

Three hundred years ago, there was a particularly bold Dutch sea captain. At sea he feared nothing and no one. His ship was swifter than anyone's else's. He was very proud of that.

While sailing around Africa, the Dutch captain's ship was caught in a sudden storm. As the storm grew worse, the crew pleaded with the captain to put into some port to ride out the weather. The captain wouldn't listen to them. He just shut himself up in his cabin, smoking his pipe. Some crewmen heard him laughing and cursing.

As the storm grew more violent, the captain came out of his cabin and screamed at the wind. He challenged the storm to do its worst. "I'll round the Cape if it takes till Judgment Day!" he shouted.

Suddenly a glowing form appeared on the deck. The crew was terrified. The captain, as usual, showed no fear. "Who wants a peaceful voyage?" he cried. "I'm asking nothing from you." He dragged his pistol from his belt. "Clear out, or I'll blow your brains out," he warned.

The form did not move. The captain aimed his pistol at the glowing figure. When he tried to fire, the pistol exploded in his hand.

The glowing figure then placed a terrible curse on the

captain. It said that he was doomed to sail the seas, without rest, forever. His phantom ship was to bring bad luck to all who sighted it.

Throughout the centuries, many sailors have reported seeing a ghostly sailing ship. The ship has been called the *Flying Dutchman*. The legend frightened sailors. In the days of wooden ships, sailing was dangerous. Sailors were afraid of anything that might bring them bad luck.

The most famous sighting of the *Flying Dutchman* came in 1881. According to a written account:

"The *Flying Dutchman* crossed our bow—a strange red light, as of a phantom ship all aglow. In the middle of the light were masts and sails. It was about two hundred yards away. When we arrived, there was no sign of a material ship. The night was clear and the sea calm. Thirteen persons altogether saw her."

The sighting was made from a ship called *The Bacchante*. The man who wrote the account would later become King George the Fifth of England. The future king did not have

any unusual bad luck. However, the first of the thirteen men to spot the phantom fell from a high mast to his death on the deck. The admiral on *The Bacchante* became very ill. He died before the ship reached port. Was this the result of the curse of the *Flying Dutchman*? One wonders.

The Bell Ringer's Ghost

In the small town of Wisbech in England, there is a house called the Elm Vicarage. It is a house that is used by the minister of the local church and his family. And it's haunted.

Hundreds of years ago there was a monastery where the house now stands. It is near the river. Today the area is safe. When the monastery was there, floods were a real danger. When a flood threatened, it was the job of one of the monks to watch the river. Before the water rose too high he was to ring a bell to warn the others. The monastery itself was often flooded. The monks needed time to get to higher ground.

One night the job of the bell ringer fell to a monk named Ignatius. While watching, he fell asleep. The floodwaters rose quickly and the sleeping Ignatius did not ring the bell. As a result, several monks were drowned. Ignatius was one of them. Since that time his spirit has haunted the area where the monastery once stood.

Ignatius is not an evil or frightening ghost. He is a helpful one. And he is usually quite polite.

People who have lived in Elm Vicarage first hear footsteps in the night. Only after a few weeks or months does Ignatius himself appear. In the beginning, the form is faint. Little by little it becomes clearer. The ghost seems to give people time to get used to him. The figure is that of a man in his mid-thirties. He has curly hair and a thin face. He is always dressed in a brown monk's robe and sandals. Those who have seen him say he looks worried.

The wife of the Reverend A. R. Bradshaw once bumped into the ghost. "Do be careful," the ghost said.

Mrs. Bradshaw's most remarkable story was about how the ghost saved her from an evil spirit. One night she awoke with a choking feeling. She saw a black shape standing over her. Two powerful hands were around her throat. She couldn't move.

She couldn't even make a noise. Her husband was asleep in the next room, but she could not call to him. Mrs. Bradshaw was sure that she was going to die.

Suddenly the spirit of Ignatius appeared. He pulled the hands away from her throat. He pushed the dark form away from her, and it vanished. Mrs. Bradshaw's throat was bruised and red, but otherwise she was unhurt.

Ignatius told her that she had been attacked by the ghost of an evil man that had been murdered in the room. He also told her that by good deeds he was trying to work off the guilt for having fallen asleep at his post. He said that one day he would find eternal peace. Then his ghost would not be seen anymore.

The Brown Lady

Many of the large old houses of England are supposed to be haunted by ghostly ladies. The ghost that haunts Raynham Hall has not only been seen, she has been photographed!

The first reports of the ghost of Raynham Hall come from 1835. Some guests were staying at the Hall over Christmas. One of the guests, a Colonel Loftus, saw a strange woman in a brown dress gliding down the hall. Before he could get a good look at her, she disappeared.

A few days later he saw the same figure again. This time he got a good look, and wished he hadn't. Her face wore a horrible grin. And where her eyes should have been there were only empty sockets. It was not a face anyone wanted to see twice.

A few years later a brave young man determined to take on the ghost. He took his pistol and went to the upstairs hall where she was often seen. He hid in a corner and waited.

Then he saw the ghostly figure gliding toward him. He took his pistol, aimed carefully, and fired. The bullet went right through the figure. The ghost just grinned horribly at him.

From the descriptions, an artist painted a picture of the ghost, popularly called *The Brown Lady*. The picture hangs in an upstairs bedroom at Raynham Hall. Only the bravest guests are willing to stay in that bedroom.

The most famous appearance of the Brown Lady came in 1936. A couple of photographers from a magazine came to the Hall to take pictures.

One of the photographers was setting up his camera to take a picture of the staircase. The other photographer saw a ghostly form coming down the stairs. He shouted to his companion to take a picture quickly. The first photographer didn't even have time to look up. He could not see what he was taking a picture of. The figure disappeared as soon as the flashgun went off. When the film was developed, there was something on the stairs that shouldn't have been there.

You can't make out details. All you can see is a shape. But more than anything else, it looks like the figure of a woman.

The Brown Lady is usually seen inside the Hall. From time to time, the phantom has been spotted on the road near the house.

No one knows who the Brown Lady is. Some think that in life she was Dorothy Walpole, sister of the powerful English politician, Sir Robert Walpole. She died in the 1730s. She had married into the Townshend family which

owned Raynham Hall. If this is so, then the ghost is a traveler. The spirit of Dorothy Walpole, dressed in brown, also haunts nearby Houghton Hall, which had been built by her brother.

Bentham's Headless Ghost

Jeremy Bentham was a famous English philosopher. He was also a little strange.

He thought everything should be useful. It was very wasteful, he said, just to bury bodies in the ground. He thought that they should be preserved and put on display. He thought it was a particularly good idea for smart fellows like himself to be put on display after death. He said that such displays would inspire the young.

So when Jeremy Bentham died in 1832, he left instructions that his body should be preserved, stuffed, and put on display in a glass case. The case was to be set up at the entrance of the University of London. It's still there.

But things didn't work out quite as Bentham had hoped. In the first place, his head wasn't very well preserved. It has been replaced by a wax model. The original skull now rests between the figure's feet.

The partially preserved philosopher doesn't inspire anyone. The display is looked upon as a gruesome oddity.

Bentham's ghost has been reported in the halls of the University. The spectre carries his skull under his arm. Sometimes, it is said, he rolls his skull down the corridors, like a bowling ball.

He was a little strange in life. He is a little strange as a ghost.

Winterton's Spirit

David Winterton had been a British soldier. After he left the army, he was never able to settle down. He traveled all over the world. He wound up living in a city in the Middle East.

Winterton's only friend was a shopkeeper named Hassan. The two men often talked about life after death. They made a pact. Whichever man died first would try to come back and contact the other.

A little while later there was a terrible epidemic. Winterton became very sick. He was rushed to the hospital. He was not expected to survive.

Hassan went to the hospital and was told his friend had died. Sadly, the shopkeeper went home. That evening the form of Winterton appeared in Hassan's room. Hassan was not surprised.

"I'm sorry you're dead, my friend," said Hassan.

"But I'm not dead," said the figure. "They only think I'm dead. I'm sure I will recover, if they don't bury me first. You must stop them. There is not much time. Please hurry, my friend."

The form then disappeared.

The next morning Hassan went to the hospital again. He found out where Winterton's body had been taken. It was a warehouse near the graveyard. There was only an aged caretaker on duty.

Hassan asked to see the body of his friend. The caretaker refused to let him in.

"Has the body been taken for burial yet?" Hassan asked.

The caretaker was uncomfortable. "To tell the truth, I'm not sure."

"What do you mean, you're not sure! Either it has or it hasn't."

"The body has disappeared," the caretaker admitted. "It was brought in yesterday, and put on a table with the others. During the evening I stepped out for some dinner. It's against the rules, I know. But you can't eat in there. I locked the door. When I came back the body was gone. No one could get in. No one would have stolen a body."

"What time did this happen?" asked Hassan.

"About seven in the evening," said the caretaker.

Hassan recalled that was about the time he saw Winterton's figure.

The caretaker said there was a small window in the room. When he went out, the window was closed. When he came back, it was open. It could only be opened from the inside. The window was just large enough for a thin man like Winterton to squeeze through.

Was Winterton alive, as the figure had said, Hassan wondered. Had he escaped through the window? If he did, he was still a very sick man wandering the streets. Perhaps he was dead already. Hassan thought that if he had listened to the spirit when it first appeared, he might have saved his old friend.

The caretaker pleaded with Hassan not to tell anyone what had happened.

"It's not your fault," said Hassan. "I'm to blame. I should have come sooner." The caretaker did not know what Hassan was talking about.

Winterton was never found, dead or alive. His spirit did not appear to Hassan again.